Ten Rules of Information Security for the Smaller Business
A Plain English Guide

Ten Rules of Information Security for the Smaller Business
A Plain English Guide

ALAN CALDER

IT Governance Publishing

IT Governance Publishing
IT Governance Limited
Unit 3, Clive Court
Bartholomew's Walk
Cambridgeshire Business Park
Ely, Cambridgeshire
CB7 4EH
United Kingdom

www.itgovernance.co.uk

© Alan Calder 2008

First published in the United Kingdom in 2008
by IT Governance Publishing

ISBN 978-1-905356-54-6

PREFACE

When you go away, leaving your house unoccupied, do you lock the front door? And do you only lock the front door, leaving lots of windows open, or do you also make sure that at least your ground floor windows are all shut and locked? What about the back door? Would you bother with an alarm? Why?

And if you were to park your car in a dodgy area, would you lock the doors before you walked away from it? Would you bother with a car alarm, or a steering wheel lock? Are there some areas where you might even want someone to stand guard over your car while you were gone?

And if you went into a shop that was advertising huge discounts on incredibly expensive sun-drenched holidays at a five star hotel in the Caribbean, and there was no till, just a man in dark glasses who wanted payment in cash – in full – today – in exchange for which he was promising to send you your tickets in a month's time, would you be likely to hand over any money at all?

Yes, the physical, analogue world has a number of fraudsters, charlatans and thieves who are keen to steal your money and your goods, and you are used to taking precautions against them. It's no different on the Internet – no more safe, and no less safe. That's important: <u>the Internet is not less safe</u> than the physical world. If you don't take appropriate precautions, you can expect – sooner or later – to pay the price. On the Internet, the bad guys are just a mouse click away – and most of the interesting and cool things to do are also not yet very secure.

You can use the Internet perfectly safely, as long as you remember to apply basic common sense, and take the basic precautions – by applying the 10 common sense rules in this book.

THE 10 RULES OF INFORMATION SECURITY:

1   Safeguard your computer.
2   Use strong passwords and a screensaver.
3   Update and patch your operating system.
4   Have an up-to-date firewall.
5   Have up-to-date anti-malware software.
6   Act anti-spam.
7   Secure wireless networks.
8   Be sensible – don't take unnecessary risks.
9   Back it up.
10 Fix problems as soon as they arise.

ABOUT THE AUTHOR

Alan Calder is a founder director of IT Governance Ltd. Before that, he was CEO of Wide Learning, a supplier of e-learning, of Focus Central London and, before that, of Business Link London City Partners (BLLCP). He was also a member of the DTI's Information Age Competitiveness Working Group. He was for many years a member of the DNV Certification Services Certification Committee, which certifies compliance with international standards including ISO27001.

Alan works with a wide range of clients on IT governance and information security projects which include design, implementation and deployment of management systems and the development and writing of white papers. He also speaks at seminars and presentations on IT governance, regulatory compliance and information security. Alan can be contacted on acalder@itgovernance.co.uk.

Books by the same author

Corporate Governance: a Practical Guide, Kogan Page (2008).

Implementing Information Security according to ISO27001, van Haren Publishing (2007).

Business Guide to Information Security, Kogan Page (2006).

Nine Steps to Success: an ISO27001 Implementation Overview, ITGP (2006).

About the Author

The Case for ISO27001, ITGP (2006).

IT Governance: Guidelines for Directors, ITGP (2005).

IT Governance Today: a Practitioner's Handbook, ITGP (2005).

Books by the same author, with Steve Watkins

IT Governance: a Manager's Guide to Data Security and ISO27001/ISO27002 (4th Edition), Kogan Page (2008).

International IT Governance: an Executive Guide to Data Security and ISO27001, Kogan Page (2007).

Information Security Risk Management for ISO27001, ITGP (2007)

CONTENTS

INTRODUCTION

We live in an analogue world and, increasingly, work, play and do business in a digital one. Our assets, the things we own in either world and that are valuable to us, are also attractive to others. As we've extended our field of activity into the digital World Wide Web (or Internet), as we've developed new technologies and acquired new skills, so we've been followed by all those antisocial elements who plagued us in the analogue one.

Over the centuries, we've become accustomed (particularly in the first world) to taking appropriate precautions around our analogue assets, health and security. We know how to secure our homes, offices and cars. We know what precautions to take while walking, shopping and doing business. We know which neighbourhoods to stay out of. We know which customers to keep an eye on, and we have well-developed police and justice systems that deal (to one extent or another) with miscreants.

Although the police and justice systems are still coming to grips with the digital world, the miscreants – criminals (of all sorts: organised, white collar and occasional), malefactors, spies and other undesirables – have already successfully adapted their modus operandi to cyberspace. Of course, that doesn't mean that they've deserted the analogue world, they've just extended their sphere of operations to the digital one. We've therefore got to get as good at dealing with the cyber threats and risks as we already are at dealing with the analogue ones.

In the same way that the average individual can understand the rules for maintaining and driving a motor car without having to be an auto-mechanic, so any business computer user can understand how to be safe online, without needing to be a computer expert. Just as you would be hard-pushed to help a medical specialist diagnose and cure an illness, without first having a good idea of what it takes to stay healthy, or what disease feels like, so it would be difficult to ensure that your business network or computer was adequately secured – or even to call in appropriate outside help – without some grasp of the basic threats.

Threats and risks

Cost-effective information security requires a combination of behaviour and tools that are appropriate and proportionate to the cyber-threats and computer-related risks that we face. Our starting point, therefore, must be to understand the threats and risks.

A threat is defined as the 'potential cause of an unwanted incident, which may result in harm to a system or organisation' and a risk as the 'combination of the probability of an event and its consequence' (both definitions are from the international information security best practice standard, ISO27001:2005). A threat and a risk are not, in other words, the same thing. There are many threats that pose no risk (for instance, the hacker threat poses no risk to someone who doesn't use a computer, and the grave cyberterrorism threat poses a limited risk to a small organisation that only uses the Internet for e-mail). Every user has to decide individually how much of a risk each threat is. Experience teaches that erring on the side of caution makes most sense.

Threats in the digital world, as in the analogue one, originate with people. These people fall into four groups:

- Criminals (thieves, fraudsters and organised crime).
- Malefactors (hackers, vandals, terrorists, cyber-warriors, some ex-employees and other disgruntled or vengeful individuals).
- Undesirables (scam artists, spammers, 'ethical' hackers and nerds).
- The incompetent, or the simply unaware (friends and family, and other third parties).

Incompetence, lack of awareness and lack of skill are similar problems in either space. The digital threats, and the type of attacks that express them, have the same sort of objectives as they do in the analogue world, but because of the nature of computers, digital data and the Internet, their characteristics are different. These characteristics, as identified by Bruce Schneier in *Secrets & Lies*, are:

- Automation: computers automate mundane tasks; illegal or destructive activity with which someone would struggle to cost-effectively achieve critical mass in the analogue world can be automated. Computers make Denial of Service attacks and large scale junk mail possible, just as they enable 100% surveillance of the Internet communications traffic of any individual or organisation.

- Data collection: digital data requires less storage space than the equivalent analogue information and can be more quickly harvested, stored and mined. What can be done will (often) be done and, as a result, massive databases of personal and commercial data now exist all over the world. They make spamming, surveillance and identity theft that much easier.

- Action at a distance: in cyberspace, the bad guys are just a mouse click away; the criminal who is trying to steal your money may be based in Chechnya, Moldavia or on a Pacific island. He will be just as effective, quick and silent as a criminal next door, far harder to trace and arrest than his analogue equivalent, and financially more successful.

- Propagation: the Web enables ideas, skills and digital tools to be shared around the world within hours. It also enables techniques to be widely replicated and a vast array of computers to be linked into any one attack.

The types of cyberspace attacks that we have to be ready to deal with are:

- Criminal attacks (fraud, theft and grand larceny, identity theft, hacking, extortion, phishing, IPR and copyright theft, piracy, brand theft, 'spoofing').

- Destructive attacks (cyberterrorism, hackers, ex-colleagues, vengeful individuals, cyberwar, cybervandals, anarchists, viruses).

- Nerd attacks (Denial of Service attacks, publicity hounds, adware).
- Espionage attacks (data theft, spyware).

These attacks affect individuals and small businesses indiscriminately. Individuals and small businesses are rarely directly or individually targeted in an attack (unless they have very substantial assets or some other significant value to the attacker), but they are nevertheless at risk in an environment where automation, action at a distance and propagation enable an attacker to successfully target a very big number of smaller fish.

Malefactors know that the majority of individuals and smaller businesses have inadequate cyber-protection and they exploit this, for instance deploying large numbers of unprotected computers in huge zombie networks, to mount large-scale Denial of Service attacks and to distribute floods of spam.

Looking ahead

- There is a strong trend toward mobile computing. The use of laptop computers, Personal Digital Assistants (PDAs), mobile phones, digital cameras, portable projectors and MP3 players has made working from home or on the road relatively straightforward, with the result that secure physical perimeters are disappearing. There are many more remote access points to networks, and the number of easily accessible endpoint devices has increased dramatically, increasing the opportunities to break into networks and steal or corrupt information.

- Better hacker tools are available every day, on hacker websites that, themselves, proliferate. These tools are improved regularly and, increasingly; less and less technologically proficient criminals – and computer literate terrorists – are thus enabled to cause more and more damage to target networks and systems.

- Increasingly, hackers, virus writers and spam operators are co-operating to find ways of spreading more spam: not just because it's fun, but because direct e-mail marketing of dodgy products is lucrative. Phishing and other Internet fraud activity continues evolving and will become an ever bigger problem.

- This will lead, inevitably, to an increase in blended threats that can only be countered with a combination of technologies and processes.

Implementation guidance

The implementation guidance for each of the 10 rules is aimed primarily at small businesses, people with a single computer installed in a small office or working from home, and at micro-businesses which, if they are operating two or more computers, are doing so either on a peer-to-peer network or on a small network with a single Internet gateway. You should apply the 10 rules to each user and computer on the network. In other words, the guidance focuses on single computers but assumes that, in multiple computer situations, you will apply it to each computer. And you will need to do this – your security is only as strong as your weakest link, and if one user (perhaps someone who only uses a computer once per week) switches off anti-virus protection or leaves a password in clear text on a website, you may never recover!

Identify your operating system

The first step is for you to identify your operating system. If your computer is a Macintosh®, go to *www.apple.com/support/security/* for further advice. The guidance in this book will continue to be useful, but specific configuration instructions will need to come from Apple.

If it is a Windows® PC, then you need to identify which version of Windows® you are running. Go to *Start*, right-click on *My Computer* – select *Properties* – then select the *General* tab, and this will show you the Windows® version you are running, together with details of the latest service pack you have installed.

The configuration steps in this guide relate to Windows® XP but the principles apply to all Windows® operating systems and the implementation steps (identified here in *italics*) for older operating systems are usually similar to those identified here. If you are not running Windows® XP, arrange to upgrade as soon as possible; the security structure of XP is so much better than anything that came before it. If you have more than one operating system running within a small office/home network, consider standardising on one: it will make life much simpler for you.

CHAPTER 1: RULE 1 – SAFEGUARD YOUR COMPUTER

1   Workstations should be set up in a secure, clean, calm, stable environment. You don't want them exposed to animals, dirt, machinery, chaos or anything else that might damage any part of the machine. You don't want it balanced on a pile of books or boxes from which it might topple.

2   Don't have (large coils of) loose cables that might be a safety hazard; tripping over a cable and pulling it out of the computer – or pulling the computer over – might not be something you want to do.

3   Always log out of and shut down Windows®, and switch your computer off when it's not in use. Don't switch your computer off without having first logged out; you may damage some programs.

4   Install an Uninterruptible Power Source (UPS). While household and office power supplies are in theory protected from power surges, they are not immune from power failure. Your UPS will save you losing your work if there is a failure. You can buy them inexpensively from computer shops and they should be designed to:

i   Deal with any mains power surges or brownouts that might harm your computer – these are called line-interactive units;

ii   Continue running for long enough, in the event of a power cut, for you to log out of and shut down your computer in an orderly way – about four minutes.

5   Ensure that your physical Internet connection (switch or modem cable) is easily accessible and clearly marked, so that you can disconnect it urgently should you need to. Make sure that it won't get easily or mistakenly disconnected by someone else. Remember: 'Always on, always vulnerable'; if you're not using the Internet but leaving your computer switched on, disconnect from the Internet; this will make it impossible for someone to access your machine remotely while you're away from it.

Security on the move

6   The biggest risk associated with laptops (also known as notebooks) is, in fact, the loss or theft of the laptop. The risks associated with the physical loss of a laptop include (but are not limited to):

i   Loss of confidential or proprietary information, which might expose you or your employer to loss of competitiveness, loss of reputation, loss of clients, loss of suppliers, compromise of business operations or of individuals, breach of stock exchange regulations affecting confidential information exposure, etc.;

ii   Loss of private information, which might expose you or your employer to breach of privacy and data protection legislation actions;

iii   Loss of irreplaceable information, which might expose you or your employer to severe disruption;

iv   Loss of confidential access information (user names, passwords), which might enable a malicious acquirer of the laptop to access and compromise (or plunder) your or your employer's resources;

v   Loss of a network authenticated device which might be used maliciously for accessing secure facilities elsewhere.

So, the physical security issues are paramount. In the office, physical security means using computer locking cables (as well as alarms (e.g. from *www.trackitcorp.com*) and tracing services for high value devices) during the day, to ensure that laptops that are in use on desks cannot simply be picked up and removed. At night, it means securing laptops in a purpose built laptop safe (see for example *www.loxit.com* for a UK supplier of a range of physical security devices for laptops) or its user removing the laptop from the premises.

Laptop physical security is, outside the office, even more difficult. In theory, laptops are safer at home (if home is occupied) than they are in an unattended office and that is probably true – as long as the laptop doesn't contain highly confidential information, in which case alternative protective measures (laptop safe) need to be taken.

No, the real problem is in transit: it's what happens to the laptop in the coffee shop, in its bag on the bus or train, or in the cab. More laptops are lost in cabs than by any other means. The basic guidance (apart from paying attention) is, firstly, to store laptops in nondescript carry bags, or inside brief cases, anything that doesn't look like a computer case, so as to avoid encouraging a passing criminal to consider stealing it.

Secondly, keep a firm hold on the laptop – in its case – at all times, especially in bars, hotels and while using public transport. When you're not using it, keep it under your feet (under the airplane seat in front of you, for instance) or on your lap. Assume that someone nearby would love to steal it.

Thirdly, do not leave a laptop unattended, not in a public place, not on view inside a vehicle, not anywhere. Keep a close eye on it when you go through a security checkpoint – someone might grab it while you're distracted by something or someone else. Don't leave it behind on the checkpoint conveyor belt because you're in a hurry. Be paranoid.

Fourthly, if you have any personal data (for instance, about staff or customers) install whole disk encryption on your laptop; this will protect your information if the laptop is stolen or lost, and may also protect you against a Data Protection Act breach. Whole disk encryption software is inexpensive and relatively easy to install; take a look, for instance, at *www.pgp.com/products/ wholediskencryption*.

Of course, you should also watch for snoops, looking over your shoulder to see your financial data before they steal the laptop. You should also ensure that your computer(s) are all appropriately covered under either (but not both, otherwise you could have a complicated claim experience) your household or your business insurance policy.

7   Pay equal care and attention to the security of your PDA and mobile telephones. While they're not as valuable as your laptop, someone will want to steal them and you're not going to enjoy dealing with this loss in a foreign country.

CHAPTER 2: RULE 2 – USE STRONG PASSWORDS AND A SCREENSAVER

1   If you use a computer on a corporate network, you will have been allocated a user name with user rights described in your access agreement. You should not disclose your user name; you should not allow anyone else to use a computer that you are already logged into, and you should never attempt to access systems or information that you are not authorised for.

2   If it is your computer, you probably log into your computer as 'administrator'. This is the most powerful class of user that can operate your computer; an administrator can change anything, delete anything, hide anything, steal anything, corrupt anything and use your computer to do anything, legal or illegal – and you'll never be able to prove it wasn't you who did it. So it's not too clever to make it even vaguely easy for just anyone passing by to log into your computer and wield this sort of power.

3   If your computer is a standalone, and kept in a relatively private area, then you should go to *User Accounts* in *Control Panel* and

    i   Use *Change an account* to change the user name from 'administrator' to your own preferred user name (how about a variant of your own name?), because this at least doesn't look quite as interesting to a potential miscreant.

    ii   Require the use of a strong password – make it something that is not easy for a miscreant to guess – so don't use consecutive letters, numbers, your birthday (or anyone else's), a family member or your dog's name, or anything equally obvious (so 'password' would be a bad choice). Don't choose a word from the dictionary (hackers use automated dictionary attacks). Use something that is at least seven characters long. Make it a mix of upper case and lower case, and mix numbers, letters and symbols. This will make it difficult for someone to guess. Don't write your password on a post-it note – or anything else – that you keep anywhere near the computer. If you think someone might have guessed it, change it (in *Change an account*). The simplest way to create a password that you can remember is to create a phrase (e.g.: 'hackers should be taken out and shot') and to use the first letters of each word as the password (e.g.: 'hsbtoas'), then building in a numeral, a change of case, and a symbol (e.g.: 'hsBtoas7$'), which probably gives you something pretty uncrackable.

4   It is particularly important that any password you use over the Web (i.e. for accessing your bank account) is a strong one.

5   By all means, use the same password for a number of sites and services – it's difficult to remember more than one or two strong passwords – but see the advice below, about disposable e-mail addresses for use on the Internet. Software and devices are available

that enable you to control and manage multiple passwords and user names.

6   Be sure to change your password, on all those websites, every three to four months – just in case someone, somewhere has intercepted a communication containing it but doesn't yet have the rest of the information necessary to do damage to you.

7   Unless you first contacted them (and you're sure you really got through to them) NEVER give your password to someone who asks for it, irrespective of the reason offered or the apparent genuineness of their credentials (including their website). If someone asks you for your password, they're up to no good. Don't give it to them. Not even if they tell you that you'll be banned from the Internet for ever and have all your money frozen.

8   If your computer is part of a small network, or kept in a busy area, or is accessible by a number of other users, or is operated by someone else in your team, particularly someone computer-savvy, you need to be more careful. Go to *User Accounts* in *Control Panel* and

   i   Carry out the steps identified in 3) above for the Administrator user name, but make the password really hard to guess. You're not going to use this account again, except for administrator functions, so file the password somewhere very safe – and nowhere near your computer.

   ii   Select the *Guest Account* and *Turn it off*. This will stop anyone that hasn't been issued a user name using this group account to access the computer without permission.

iii *Create a New Account*, using a variant of your own name for the user name, make it a *Limited Account*, and make it password protected, following the guidance of 3i) above. This is the account that, in future, you should use for all your computer activity.

iv If someone else is going to use your computer, create a separate user account for that person, following the guidance above. Whenever you are going to change computer user, have one user log out as a user before the other user logs in.

9 Set up a password-protected screensaver in *Display Properties* (in *Control Panel*); choose a delay before the screensaver operates (10 minutes is probably practical) and tick the *On resume, password protect* box. You can even choose what the screensaver looks like. You can now be sure that, if you walk away from your machine without logging off, it will automatically protect itself from access by a miscreant taking advantage of the fact that you are already logged in. When you return, you type in your password (the one you set in 3i) above) and you're back in business.

CHAPTER 3: RULE 3 – UPDATE AND PATCH YOUR OPERATING SYSTEM

1   One reason why there are so many viruses and hackers out there is that Microsoft's Windows® product is so widely distributed. It does have faults – the consequence of ever more complex code, with ever more sophisticated features, rushed out as fast as possible. It's also a consequence of its widespread use: hackers target the most commonly used software, not the least used. Some people recommend installing some other operating system – anything but Microsoft®. There is an argument in favour of installing some browser other than Internet Explorer® (such as Firefox) and some e-mail package other than Outlook® or Outlook® Express (such as Eudora® or Thunderbird™). We don't think it's necessary, but you really have to make your own decisions, particularly around browsers and e-mail. We do think that, if you are running a small network, you should standardise on one application. We think that Microsoft® has all the features, pretty well everyone else is using their software and, after all, you already know how to use it – you just want to do so securely. That means patching the holes and updating the software as often as you can.

2   Microsoft release hot fixes, patches and upgrades to their software as and when vulnerabilities are identified and they've adequately tested the new code. Hot fixes are

released as soon as possible, once a significant vulnerability is identified; patches are released on a standard monthly cycle, and service packs are released about once per year. Service packs make improvements as well as consolidating previous patches and hot fixes, but that is not a reason to delay updating until the upgrade arrives, because you probably won't survive uninfected and un-hacked for that long. Service Pack 3 (SP3) was the most recent service pack available for Windows® XP at the time this book went to press.

3   Log   your   computer   on   to
http://update.microsoft.com/microsoftupdate/v6/ default.aspx?ln=en-us, which can automatically scan your computer to see what updates are required; ask it to identify which high priority updates are required. It will produce a list of the available updates. Follow the on-screen instructions to download and install them. It would be sensible to ensure (if you use dial-up access), before you start any downloads, that your telephone access will not be interrupted until you have finished the download and you might need to consider, if you don't have a broadband or ISDN connection, having Microsoft mail very big updates (service packs, for instance) to you on a CD-ROM – or you may be online for an expensive few hours while the download runs its course.

4   Once you know that your computer is running a fully updated version of the operating system, keep it that way. Windows® XP (also Windows® 2000 with SP3 and Windows® Me) all support automatic updates, a feature that

automatically checks for the availability of updates whenever you are online and downloads them to your computer for you to install. You do have to configure this feature – in *System Properties*, where you want to tick the setting that downloads updates automatically, doesn't install them but alerts you (with a balloon at the bottom of your screen) so that you can. This does give you the option, if you have an urgent task to complete immediately after logging on, to do that before you commence installation; an automatic update might significantly affect your ability to carry out any other task in parallel.

5   Keep yourself informed: Microsoft provides an e-mail update service that provides non-technical alerts for users about security issues and software updates. Register for the newsletter:
www.microsoft.com/protect/secnews/default.mspx.

6   You should also update and patch your applications; if you are running Microsoft® Office®, go to the Office® (*http://office.microsoft.com*) page, click *Check for Updates* and arrange to have any identified updates installed. These are less important (but not much) than Windows® updates and patches.

CHAPTER 4: RULE 4 – HAVE AN UP-TO-DATE FIREWALL

1   A firewall is essential for any computer – and needs to be either on the network gateway, or on the computer – and, in certain situations (e.g. when working wirelessly and/or mobile), on both.

2   Of course, you can't think why anyone should attack your machine – but it's the automated hacks that will do the damage – who wants their computer to be a part-time member of a massive zombie network used for distributed denial of service attacks, spam distribution or illegal data storing? You're in slightly less danger if you use a dial-up connection than if you have a (permanently on) broadband one; this is because, although your IP address is permanent if you are on broadband and changes every time you log-on with dial up, the whole global range of IP addresses can be scanned and checked by an automated hack or worm every 15 minutes. You probably don't want to risk someone else seeing any of your financial transactions or accessing your private data (e.g. bank records).

3   If you are operating a small network with a single Internet gateway (such as on a wireless modem, for instance), you will need to install a firewall on the gateway. Internet modems should come with pre-installed firewalls.

4   You need to install a personal firewall on standalone computers, on each computer in a peer-to-peer network and also on each

computer in a small, single server network. Installing a firewall is not rocket science. Microsoft® XP (SP1 +) provides a default firewall which is dependable. Even Microsoft doesn't pretend, though, that their firewall is a replacement for good third party products. There are a number of available firewalls, some free, others not. There are a number of criteria to consider in choosing a firewall (including integration with anti-virus software, instant messaging protection, etc.), and these should be considered. Don't think 'free' as a long-term solution.

5   You need to have updated your anti-virus protection, and run an anti-virus system scan before you download or start installing your firewall.

6   BEFORE you download a third party firewall, you need to turn off the Microsoft® XP default firewall. Two firewalls DO NOT equal twice as much protection: they equal a false sense of security and NO PROTECTION! Go to *Control Panel – Windows Firewall* and tick the *Off, not recommended* button. Don't hang around now; go get the third party product you've already chosen.

7   If you are running on a broadband connection, you need to test your firewall; online services are available that will carry out inexpensive penetration tests and you should test your firewall immediately after installation and on a monthly basis (or after any significant software changes) thereafter.

8   You also need to keep your firewall up to date; your firewall software and supplier should

have an automatic update feature that will alert you to needed updates and download them for you as and when they become available.

9 You should familiarise yourself with the basics of your firewall, rather as you familiarise yourself with the basics of car maintenance or home security. You will have a few new things to do, including responding to alerts and allowing both incoming and outgoing Internet activity (because, for instance, if your firewall alerts you to all outgoing activity, it's sure to detect a Trojan phoning home), and there may be minimal set-up decisions to make when you install the product. Follow the online 'help' instructions provided (usually, the default option is adequate) or contact the provider's helpdesk.

CHAPTER 5: RULE 5 – HAVE UP-TO-DATE ANTI-MALWARE SOFTWARE

1   There are some 200,000 viruses, worms and Trojans circulating in the wild. Some of them are worse than others, and some are very nasty indeed. Spyware, adware and other 'free' programs are also part of the problem. You must install anti-malware software, both to protect your computer from infection and to stop your computer infecting others.

2   Your Internet Service Provider (ISP) should have anti-virus software installed at its Internet gateway, and this should catch the majority of virus traffic. It is not foolproof and you don't want to rely on it alone.

3   You need to install anti-malware software on standalone computers and on each computer in a peer-to-peer network. You need to have anti-malware software even if you only use Web mail. Don't bother trying to find free stuff; anything that's any good costs money to keep up to date. Anti-virus software has to do many things, not the least of which is catching and eliminating today's new viruses, worms and blended threats. It also has to integrate with your firewall and spam filter, find viruses that might have come in via Instant Messenger, on a CD-ROM or on a USB stick, or on an e-mail downloaded from a Web mail account. This means that you probably want an integrated anti-virus and firewall product. Anti-virus software must come from a reputable supplier and must be the latest version of their software.

4   You should run only one anti-virus package; two or more will conflict and slow your machine down. If you are changing anti-virus suppliers, uninstall your current package (*Control Panel – Add or Remove Programs*) before installing the new one.

5   Once you have chosen, and installed, an anti-virus software package, familiarise yourself with it, in much the same way as you familiarise yourself with how to maintain (oil, water, petrol, etc.) your motor car. Ensure that the software is up to date and is set to automatically update itself (preferably) daily. Weekly is no good. New viruses appear every day. Weekly updates are like closing the stable door after the horse has left the country. Daily is just about enough.

6   Run a complete system scan (following the instructions that come in your product's control panel); this may take about an hour, but you want to be sure that any known viruses on your system are identified and quarantined before you go any further.

7   Your vendor probably produces a virus-warning and update newsletter; register for it and pay attention to its advice. Some viruses propagate around the world before the anti-virus companies have produced a defence against them, and you want to find out that there's a problem before it's too late.

8   DON'T fall for virus hoaxes – these are usually in the form of an e-mail telling you to watch out for a particular virus and recommending that you pass the e-mail on to

everyone you know. Don't. If it is a virus, it will already have been described in that newsletter service from your vendor; you don't want to be guilty of forwarding a whole load of spam, do you?

9   DON'T open e-mail attachments (including .txt ones, and especially not anything with an .exe, .scr or .pif extension) from people you don't know or which you don't specifically recall asking to have sent to you. Be particularly careful of 'zipped' files. DON'T open files sent to you in Instant Messenger, unless you know the sender and really, really need to open their file. Chances are, it'll contain a virus that your anti-virus software won't have the opportunity to detect until after it's downloaded to your computer.

10 Spyware and adware are different from viruses and hackers. Adware is pop-up advertising software that has downloaded to, and runs on, your computer, usually without your active consent or knowledge. It will keep a series of advertisement windows open in front of you, irrespective of your attempts to close them. You may have agreed to the installation (by clicking the '*I agree*' declaration when downloading, for instance, a peer-to-peer tool) and sometimes it is contained within some shareware, freeware or other plug-in (for instance, an animated cursor) you downloaded, or was triggered by an advert you clicked. Spyware is software you didn't deliberately install, that collects information about you (for instance, by logging your keystrokes when you type passwords) and sends it across the

Internet to some third party – who might then use the information to de-fraud you or simply to send you targeted advertisements ('trackware').

11 Both adware and spyware consume substantial amounts of Central Processing Unit (CPU) power, slow your machine down, bombard you with pop-ups that get in your way, alter websites you visit, sometimes crash your computer and generally make life a bore – as well as bringing an increasing torrent of spam to your inbox. You really want to keep adware and spyware to a minimum.

12 Keep away from the more unsavoury websites and follow the advice below.

13 The first step is to clean up your machine. Download the free Microsoft® Windows® Defender program from *www.microsoft.com/downloads*, install and run it. The installation process takes about 15 minutes, but if you just follow the instructions it can be completed painlessly. Configure it for automatic updates, and for real time protection. Once it is installed, have it run a complete disk scan and then follow the advice it gives you about any adware or spyware it detects. Unless you have a good reason for retaining anything it detects (a good reason might be that a shareware/freeware program you genuinely want to retain requires you to live with the adware), remove it.

14 If you are unable to clean up your computer (i.e. in spite of installing all updates, running Windows® Defender and a virus scan, your

machine is still not working properly), you may have a more serious problem.

15 Once you have a clean machine, avoid further infestation.

16 Don't download shareware, freeware or other plug-ins unless you really know and trust the company that produced them and you have some evidence that they don't come with a payload. Read the End User Licence Agreement (EULA) and any other documentation that exists to establish the integrity of the supplier.

17 Don't install a dialler, even if it says it's for free – it probably isn't. The actual expense may be much more than you bargained for. In any case, you are already connected to the Internet. If you can only get to that site by downloading their dialler, just forget it!

18 Don't close any window or website by pressing a button that says 'agree' or 'OK' as this may also download something to your computer – ALWAYS click the red 'x' in the top right hand corner of the window to close it.

19 Don't allow just any website to install cookies on your computer: in Internet Explorer®, choose *Tools – Internet Options – Privacy* then set the slider to at least *medium*; if you're particularly paranoid, set it to *high* and see how well that works for you. Note that the default setting for Windows® XP SP2 is *medium*.

20 Don't click on links in Instant Messenger or in chat rooms, unless you know and trust the

person who sent it to you, and you really, really need to follow the link – it might take you to a (spoofed) website that installs adware, spyware or something even nastier.

21 If you really, really do want to go to a site for which someone has sent you the link, and you are a bit suspicious of it, then type the URL into the browser window, rather than clicking the link – it is possible to spoof a link.

22 Keep Windows® Defender up to date (set it for automatic updates), and be sure to run a system scan on a regular basis: at least once per month. The Microsoft® product will do it every day.

CHAPTER 6: RULE 6 – ACT ANTI-SPAM

1   Spam is e-mail that you don't want, that clogs your inbox, trying to sell you all sorts of things that you don't need. It is bulk e-mail, sent by someone you don't know, and it may be commercial, political, religious, fraudulent or simply malicious in nature. You don't want to read it. You really don't. There's a lot of it about: some estimates are that more than 80% of all e-mail is now spam.

2   There is also bulk e-mail that you DO want to receive and, because you want to receive it, it isn't spam. A spam filter is software that tries to sort the spam from the ham: to identify and block incoming spam but let through what you do want to receive.

3   Major ISPs (AOL, Yahoo, MSN®, BT Openworld, etc.) all provide gateway spam filters but, of course, they won't always correctly identify individual messages: some that shouldn't get through will, and others that should reach you, won't.

4   You want to ensure that any e-mail that does reach your computer is sorted, with the stuff you want going into your inbox and the stuff you don't want going into your junk mail box. This means that you need to have spam filtering software on your computer as well as whatever exists for the ISP and it requires that you set specific rules for your spam filter, so that it knows what you want to have excluded.

5   The major ISPs provide inbox level spam filters for webmail services as well as the

gateway ones and, if you use one of these ISPs, you should use this facility to set the level of filter that you require. You may need to use trial and error until you get something that works for you.

6   Outlook® 2003 has an inbuilt junk mail filter. You set it by going to the Outlook® toolbar, choosing *Tools – Options – Preferences – Junk e-mail* and then choosing the level of protection that you prefer. You should probably not have stuff automatically deleted, as the filter may filter out e-mails you actually want to see. You should check the junk mail folder from time to time, identify e-mails that have been incorrectly filtered, add the sender to your *safe senders' list,* by right-clicking on the e-mail and, from the drop-down menu, choosing *Junk e-mail – Add sender to safe senders' list* (or you could choose any of the other options available).

7   A number of anti-virus packages come with spam filters. You should be wary of running more than one spam filter on your computer at a time, because the complication of getting two sets of filter rules configured correctly is probably not worth the effort. If you're running Outlook® 2003, you're probably adequately protected, so disable any other filters. There's no need, though, to worry about the two conflicting and providing no filtration between them.

8   Make sure that spammers can't get your e-mail address. DON'T:

   i   Let anyone get your real e-mail address. If you're going to leave an e-mail address on lots of websites, in chat groups and chat rooms, then get a disposable e-mail address (e.g. from hotmail – perhaps a different one for each activity) and then replace it every now and then. Whatever happens, don't leave your real e-mail address for a spammer's spambot to find.

ii   Leave ticked those boxes that say it's OK for a vendor and all its partners to send you information.

iii   Ever respond to spam – if you do, even to say 'Go Away', it proves you exist and may be gullible and so will raise you up the target list. Don't try and unsubscribe from a spam e-mail – it also has the effect of proving your existence and possible naivety. It's simpler to set your spam filter to block the sender completely ('blacklisting').

iv   Ever open spam; unless you know and trust the sender, assume that any junk e-mail message may also have a payload, such as a virus or a piece of spyware or adware – or that opening it may just send a message to the sender that you exist and are possibly gullible.

v   Let your e-mail address list in Outlook® get out of date; remove people you don't want to correspond with but do add those you do want to hear from. It helps your filter know what it should let through ('whitelisting').

9   Another option is to use 'disposable' e-mail addresses.

See *www.spamhelp.org/services/listings/verification* for information about providers of this service. It can be time consuming, though.

CHAPTER 7: RULE 7 – SECURE WIRELESS NETWORKS

The explosive proliferation in laptops, PDAs, cell phones and wireless networks has given individuals greater flexibility, enabled businesses to be more responsive, driven down their operational costs, and improved both productivity and competitiveness. Deploying a wireless network is quicker and substantially less expensive (or intrusive) than deploying traditional cabling.

Of course, as wireless communication becomes an increasingly substantial part of the economic infrastructure, so it is becoming an increasingly worthwhile target for hackers, virus writers, and organised crime. Information assets (and information is an asset because it is valuable to you – and, therefore, to others) are at ever greater risks because more and more of the technology in which they are housed and communicated is vulnerable and insecure.

Wireless networking is relatively easy: a child can set up a mobile phone or PDA out of the box, a first time computer user can log onto a Starbucks wireless Access Point (AP) using a modern laptop computer and anyone even minimally competent at basic DIY can set up a wireless network, in as long as it takes to plug in a few wireless cards and run some simple software. There's nothing to it, you just get on with it, assuming that there are no vulnerabilities, threats or potentially serious impacts to worry about.

But there are. Generally speaking, wireless local area networks (or 'WLANs') are so insecure that they are easier to break into than fixed-link, cabled local area networks (LANs) – but the information on the WLAN is just as valuable as that on the more traditional cabled network.

As an individual user of a wireless laptop – either in the home or using a public HotSpot – everything on your computer (everything) may be accessible to an outsider; and 'accessible' means, in this case, that it's as easy as simply opening and reading any of your folders and files without you being aware of it.

And any organisation that deploys a WLAN is exposed – completely – by any 'rogue user' who brings an insecure wireless computer into the office (or, more terrifyingly, a branch office) and uses it to connect to the secure office network; the network is as vulnerable as its least secure point and the network security staff are unlikely even to be aware of the 'rogue user' – until it's much too late.

The keys to wireless security are encryption and authentication. A secure WLAN will have addressed both. Small businesses that set up WLANs need to set them up properly

Encryption

Two types of encryption are available for 802.11 WLANs: Wired Equivalent Protocol ('WEP') and WiFi Protected Access ('WPA'), a more secure version of the 802.11 standard. WEP has a number of very well-known holes in it. It is better than nothing, but wireless equipment is delivered without even being WEP-enabled.

If your hardware supports both types of encryption, you should apply WPA. If it only supports WEP, and if two WEP keys are available, choose the 104-bit key. If only the 40-bit key is available, go for that. Above all, enable encryption on the laptop and on your AP.

Authentication

Authentication is the process of establishing that users are who they claim to be. It requires users to provide a combination of a user name and one or more credentials: something known (a password), something possessed (digital signatures, smart cards), or a physical feature (biometrics). Weak authentication requires just a password; strong authentication ('two factor' authentication) requires at least two of these three types of credential.

You should ensure that your wireless laptop (and your PDA) is protected by strong authentication methods. Under no circumstances should you be using a computer that doesn't have a proper username, with a strong password.

Upgrading to WPA

Businesses and individuals should upgrade to WPA as soon as possible and be alert for future upgrade options.

It is an all-or-nothing option: either everything on the WLAN is WPA-enabled or nothing is. This means that, in a small network, every wireless device (including routers, printers, game stations, etc.) must be upgraded to WPA and must support Windows® Connect Now, a feature of Windows® XP SP2 that automates WLAN configuration.

The first step, therefore, is to establish if upgrades are available (as downloads, from the websites of each device's manufacturer) for each device connected to the WLAN. If not, you will have to replace the product(s) with newer, WPA-enabled equipment. The WiFi Alliance website provides details of products that it has certified as having met the WPA standard and which are therefore interoperable. If it is not possible to upgrade all the hardware that uses the WLAN to WPA, it will unfortunately be necessary to stick with WEP and all the risks associated with it.

Windows® XP SP2 supports WPA, so any computer using that as an operating system will be ready for a WPA-enabled WLAN.

Once upgrades or replacements have been identified for each device on the WLAN, deploy them. Start by upgrading the router or other wireless AP and then upgrade all the other devices that will run on the WLAN. Once all the devices are capable of supporting WPA, it is very easy to set up a secure wireless network.

Automated WPA Wireless Network Configuration

In Windows® XP SP2, the Wireless Network Setup Wizard guides the user through all the steps necessary to configure a secure network. This methodology is adequate for both a small enterprise deployment and for a home network. A

USB flash stick is also required. The wizard can be run on any computer that will access the WLAN and it will create settings that it will write to the USB flash stick for transfer to every other device that is required to access the WLAN. Full, step-by-step instructions are available at: *www.microsoft.com/technet/community/columns/ cableguy/cg0604.mspx*, but the wizard is very straightforward. The key choices to be made during the process are:

1 To choose and assign a network name, or Service Set Identifier ('SSID'), that will not obviously identify the physical location of the AP to a war driver.

2 Choose *Use WPA Encryption.*

3 Choose *Use a USB flash drive.*

After that, simply follow the instructions, inserting the USB flash stick into each of the devices (starting with the wireless AP) so that they can automatically be configured to match the initial configuration and connect to the WLAN.

Network Magic™

The availability of a software package called 'Network Magic™' has simplified home and small office computer networking. This is available from *www.purenetworks.com* and, once downloaded onto the devices that are to form part of the small network, enables them to be quickly and easily networked together. It does not require all devices to be running Windows® XP SP2; it simplifies network creation, rather than deploying a WPA-enabled network. It has useful security features, including the capacity to identify intruders on the network.

Manual WPA Wireless Network Configuration

There are a number of situations in which it may be necessary to manually configure the network. Using the Windows® XP SP2 Wireless Network Setup Wizard, there is a prompt to print out the wireless network settings so that they can be programmed into each device manually.

If your computer infrastructure is such that it is not possible to configure a secure wireless network using Microsoft® Wizard, or Network Magic™, you are likely to need specialist assistance. You should get it.

WiFi and HotSpot security

While an increasing number of public HotSpots are deploying WPA connection software, many others (including those set up by corporations for their visitors) are likely to open. In other words, they are configured with no or minimal security, in order to 'make it easy' for users – and attackers. WPA will probably be set to 'off'. Any user who connects to a HotSpot should assume they are operating unsecured on an unsecured network. You might not be, but that's the way to think.

Clearly, wherever possible, a WPA service should be used, even if there is a cost implication. (Most mobile phone providers now also offer their own secure HotSpot technologies.) There are some essential safety precautions you should take if you are using an open HotSpot AP:

- If possible, designate the HotSpot network as an untrusted or Internet zone network in your laptop firewall settings (you must have a firewall) – the firewall may be able to detect that the network is a HotSpot one and make these changes automatically;

- Turn off file and printer sharing – otherwise anyone else using the HotSpot or with a wireless device in the vicinity can easily access data on your computer;

- Any folders containing confidential or sensitive information on your laptop should already be (strong) password-protected (and preferably encrypted);

- Use a Virtual Private Network (VPN) for communicating any confidential information across the Internet;

- Be careful about what else you do and what information you key in – for instance, ensure that any confidential information (e.g. credit card details) only gets entered into a site that uses SSL (see below) technology;

- Encrypt any e-mail (through the options button in the Outlook® e-mail toolbar, where you can set the security at the individual message level quickly and easily) that you want to keep confidential.

VPNs

A Virtual Private Network ('VPN') is a method of providing a secure computing connection across the Internet, between for instance, a home office and an office network. There are a growing number of VPN clients available and you should search the Internet for one that suits your needs and budget. One option is to sign up for a personal level VPN client, such as the one (at the moment, uniquely) provided by HotSpotVPN. Users can sign up, download and install this from *www.hotspotvpn.com*. Remember that HotSpotVPN only provides a VPN between the PDA and the HotSpotVPN servers; communications thereafter are unclear. This option is ideal for individuals and has potential cost advantages for organisations with small numbers of users who might otherwise use the Internet for normal communications without deploying a VPN.

Secure corporate mobile connection services are offered by mobile phone companies. These are particularly useful for smartphones, and will need to be appropriately configured on notebooks and may need some installation on the corporate network, if that is relevant. Contact your mobile phone provider for details of the service they offer; this will need to be installed before anyone starts travelling.

3G data cards installed into laptops, also provide a secure alternative to HotSpot technology, but the product will need to be acquired and the account set up (and some practise gained) before you start travelling.

Any VPN user names should be different from your e-mail address – your e-mail address is easy for an attacker to obtain (e.g. from a business card) – and that only leaves the password to crack. So, also apply a strong password to your VPNs (seven or more alphanumeric characters, including symbols and changes of case) – just like you do to your desktop or laptop computer.

CHAPTER 8: RULE 8 – BE SENSIBLE – DON'T TAKE UNNECESSARY RISKS

Be alert – pay attention – be sensible

1. As we said at the beginning, the bad guys are just a mouse click away from you. You'll be fine, as long as you take sensible precautions.

2. Ensure that you apply and follow the '10 rules' – and it's the first seven that are particularly important!

3. When you're surfing the Web, pay attention: if a website asks you for personal information of any sort, be very careful about providing it; if you're offered a cool piece of software, be very wary about downloading it; when you do want to buy something, be sure that your vendor is genuine and likely to deliver what you think you're buying.

4. Assume that, if you're on a questionable site, the chances of something going wrong are much greater: for instance, you're much less likely to tell your spouse, friends and children about having your credit card details ripped off if you were on a porn site than if you were on Amazon.com.

5. Good sites can sometimes also give you problems: if someone has hi-jacked the site and is using it to take advantage of a current flaw in your software, you may be caught.

6. If something starts going wrong while you're on the Internet, or on a website, hit the STOP button. Your browser should have such a button, so find it and know how to use it. If

you want even faster disconnection, pull out the cable that connects you to the Internet. Once you're safe, figure out what happened, fix it and install whatever future protection you need to avoid a repeat (see Rule 9), and only once you're clean and safe should you venture back onto the Internet.

7   Another basic rule of life also applies: 'if it looks as though it's too good to be true, it probably is'. Everything has a price, even if you can't see it right now – the real price might be the theft of your identity, followed by all your money.

E-cards

8   Online greeting cards are fun, and quite often are free. You can send them for birthdays, anniversaries, and lots more. Therefore you should also worry about them.

9   As a sender, you should assume that any information you include in an e-card can be accessed by an unscrupulous third party – so don't include any information that you would rather keep private.

10   As a recipient, you should assume that an e-card might hide some form of malware, so the basic rule about not opening an attachment from someone you don't know, or which you aren't expecting, still applies. So, even if the card is from someone you know, but it's not your birthday, don't go there.

File sharing

11 Peer-to-peer networks provide opportunities for files on your computer to be shared by other users. You might be happy with this; on the other hand, you might be concerned about someone else being able to change, delete, add to or corrupt data in the files on your computer, or about the fact that file sharing is a straightforward way for viruses to spread.

12 Disable file sharing: *Start – Settings – Network Connections – LAN* or *High Speed Internet*; then right click on each icon and, in the *Connection Properties* dialogue box, <u>unclick</u> *File and printer sharing*.

13 If you are using a file sharing system to try and get round copyright law for online music sharing and purchases, you shouldn't.

Identity theft

14 This is a relatively straightforward crime: if someone can establish themselves as you, they could borrow a large amount of money that you would then have to repay, spend all the money you've actually got, and perhaps even sell your assets for you – your house, for instance. Before you worry about the house, you should worry about the debts and credit card bills that will ruin your credit rating for ever – because, even once you've proved that it wasn't really you who incurred them, chances are they will still be sitting on your credit file.

8: Rule 8 – Be Sensible – Don't Take Unnecessary Risks

15 What does someone need in order to pretend they're you? Well, your name, address, date of birth and some proof of identity – usually a combination of credit card and utility bills. And where's the best place to get all of this? The documentary stuff comes from your rubbish bin (particularly easy if you send the discarded stuff off for re-cycling) and the date of birth from an online CV, from a social website (MySpace, Linked In or similar) from an online genealogical/family tree activity, or from some form of social engineering attack ('You may have won a huge prize, if you were born on the right day! What's your date of birth? Oh dear, that's not the one we're looking for.').

16 There are some very simple rules:

i   Buy a shredder (less that £70 from almost any stationery shop) and USE it – after all, that's what the people who send you those documents say you should do with them!

ii Don't put your date of birth in an online CV at a recruitment site (in these officially non-ageist days, it shouldn't be necessary anyway).

iii Don't put your date of birth into any 'family history' online search.

iv Don't fall for any of the social engineering attacks. Nothing is for free – especially not money.

v   Keep a close eye on what happens to any official documentation – driver's licence, passport – if anyone's desire to look at it seems unusual (particularly abroad – remember that foreigners are usually seen as easy prey, because they don't really know what's going on and they're going home shortly anyway) – assume it is – this is just another form of a social engineering attack.

Internet cafés and other public computers

17 Public computers could have keystroke loggers or other spyware that has been physically installed; someone could snoop and, when you leave the computer, someone else could find out where on the Internet you've been. Any of these possibilities risk your bank account being cleared out, your credit card details stolen, or your files and folders accessed.

18 So, be sensible. When you're using a public computer (particularly abroad):

i   Don't save log-in information: log out of websites by pressing 'logout' rather than closing the window, and disable any 'automatic log-in' options.

ii Don't enter sensitive information (e.g. credit card details, passwords in full) onto public computers, unless you're entering them into secure (SSL) sites.

iii Watch out for snoops (people reading over your shoulder) and don't leave the computer unattended (to get a coffee, for instance) with sensitive or confidential information on the screen – log out, or have a (real) friend stand guard.

iv   On completion, erase your tracks. In Internet Explorer®, click *Tools – Internet Options – General*, then

Temporary Internet files – Delete cookies and then *Delete files*, then

History – Clear history.

Online auctions

19 Online auctions are run by companies such as eBay. Research the auction site: ensure that it is genuine, reputable, that its dispute resolution policies are robust and look for guarantees that you will be refunded if you have been scammed. Don't be attracted off-site to do a deal with someone who can offer you 'something better for a direct trade' – this person will almost certainly scam you.

20 Research the seller: ensure that there is a telephone number (that works) rather than just a PO Box, and look for some evidence that the seller has done business before.

21 Research the item: is it likely to be genuine or, if it appears to be very cheap, is it likely to be a copy, imitation, fake or stolen? Remember, if it's too good to be true, it probably is.

22 Research the proposed delivery method and timetable: if it's not going to be shipped virtually immediately, assume the vendor wants some time to disappear with your money.

23 Research the proposed payment method: use an online payment service, follow the

guidance about payment options in 20 above, and question any changes in payment address made after completion of the bidding.

24 Never respond to phishing requests to update your personal details.

Online charities

25 An e-mail from an online charity, asking you to give generously (using your credit card, for instance) might be genuine – or it might be looking for the opportunity to clean out your finances. Be particularly wary about these approaches, particularly around newspaper headline disasters.

26 If you do want to donate to the charity, type its name into Google (or another search engine) and go to the real site.

Online payment services

27 Online payment services can all be used to pay safely for goods and services – although you should always be wary of a phishing site posing as one of these.

28 Remember that, if you use your credit card to fund your PayPal account, your card company will treat that single transaction as the only one it has liability for, so that any later payments out of your PayPal account that are disputed will have to be resolved with PayPal directly. The basic rule is, always, to expose as little money at a time as you have to.

8: Rule 8 – Be Sensible – Don't Take Unnecessary Risks

Online recruitment services

29 These are an ideal hunting ground for identity thieves. You should:

   i   Be prudent in how many sites you put your CV on.

   ii   Limit the information you provide: for instance, don't include your date of birth, age or home address, and consider using a temporary e-mail address only for CVs.

Online shopping

30 The safest methods of payment are, in order from best to worst, credit card – and then there's a big gap, followed by: debit card, digital wallet, cheque and, worst of all, cash. This is because you can at least dispute a transaction on your credit card statement before it is due for payment whereas, if you have already parted with the money, it is somewhat harder to get it back. Credit card companies also offer liability limitation policies for fraudulent purchases – you need to know what your own card company's policy is.

31 Online stores are usually, but not always, legitimate; certainly, the more mainstream the product, the more likely they are to be above board. You should be careful about doing business for the first time with any online store – you don't want to provide your personal and credit card details to a fraudster.

32 Check the 'Contact Us' pages. You want to find a street address and a telephone number

that you can call and arrange for a catalogue or something to be sent to you that proves the firm really exists. You also want to be doing business with a company that is based in a jurisdiction whose laws you respect and under which you might be able to take action, so compare the country shown as being the physical address of the organisation with the jurisdictional details contained in the Terms of Business posted on the website. No Terms of Business? No business.

33 You also want to find a 'privacy policy' on the site. Read it: are you happy with the arrangements the website is making to protect your privacy?

34 The danger really comes when you enter your details to purchase something. If payment is taken through an online payment service, you're relatively safe. If the online store is taking your details directly, you want to be sure that you are entering information into a secure site (look for a change in the URL to one that begins https – there should also be a small locked padlock in the bottom right hand bar of your browser), and make sure that you don't provide anything more than is essential – your mother's maiden name, for instance, would not be essential.

35 Look for a 'trustworthy website' certificate. A number of organisations offer this type of certificate; their standards and usefulness vary, so the basic rule is to click on the certificate, or otherwise trace it back to the issuing authority, and satisfy yourself as to the validity

and value of the certificate before using the website.

PDAs and mobile phones

36 Viruses now exist for mobile phones and PDAs. Bluetooth enables a third party to access your mobile telephone numbers. Both PDAs and mobile phones carry lots of data that, if lost, could inconvenience or hurt you.

37 Think about passwords and keyboard locks for both.

Phishing

38 Phishing is an online scam designed to get personal information, such as credit card details, bank account numbers, passwords, etc. – online identity theft. The miscreant sends out spam, providing a link to what looks very much like a genuine website (but is in fact a spoofed one), asking you to provide updated personal details.

39 The most important rule is: never respond to these e-mails. No reputable organisation will ever send you an e-mail asking you to update your personal information. None – not ever. If you are in doubt, phone the institution (get their telephone number from some source other than the e-mail).

40 If you think you won't be able to resist going to one of these sites, even though you know that your financial institution will NEVER, not UNDER ANY CIRCUMSTANCES ask you to

visit a site and input key details like your user name and password, then at least get yourself a 'truth bar' – an Internet browser bar that will tell you where the website you are visiting is actually located, how long ago it was set up, etc. – this will at least enable you to worry about why your apparently reputable London bank only set its website up yesterday in a middle-Eastern country. If, after this, you still choose to give them your critical personal details, please expect to lose all your money.

41 Before entering any confidential information into a website, check that it is a secure site: the Web address should start with https and there should be a locked padlock in the bottom right hand corner of the browser. Double-click this icon to see the security certificate and confirm that the name on the certificate matches that of the business whose site you think you're visiting.

42 Check your credit card and other statements. Investigate anomalies immediately. Report suspected abuses to your financial institution, to the police and, if possible, to the company whose website may have been spoofed.

Scams, frauds, 419s

43 These do happen on the Internet. Read the advice contained elsewhere in Rule 8 to remain safe and secure.

44 A 419 (or Nigerian Advance Fee) scam is one that offers to make you millions of pounds richer if you would just help out a poor

bureaucrat somewhere with your bank account details, or a small sum of money, so that they can get things moving. If it's too good to be true, it probably is.

Spoofed e-mail addresses and websites

45 Spoofing is making a transmission look like it came from someone else, or a website look like a reputable one.

46 E-mail 'returned to sender' with an attachment – and which you don't recall sending – might be spoofed, with a virus. Don't open the attachment.

47 A Web link sent to you (in spam, or by someone you don't know) might be to a spoofed site, which downloads bad stuff onto your computer or gives you an opportunity to give away all your critical information (phishing). Don't click the link. If you must, then type the URL into your Web browser. Then check the site out very carefully, particularly if it claims to be a financial services site.

CHAPTER 9: RULE 9 – BACK IT UP

1   The worst thing that can happen to you is that you lose everything on your computer. This could be because of a major system crash, a major malware intrusion, or some other disaster. You need to have copies of everything available so that you can recover yourself.

2   What's on your computer is, essentially, stored in two sorts of folders: program folders and information folders.

3   CD-ROM copies of everything in the program folders should have been supplied when you purchased the computer and you want those, and the system documentation, in a safe place.

4   You should keep a paper list of any shareware/freeware or other programs (for instance, firewall, anti-virus, etc.) that you have installed, together with website and purchase details, so that you can re-install them when you need to.

5   If you don't have important information stored in computer documents, you don't need to back it up.

6   If you do have important information on your computer, you have to make back-up copies of the relevant folders. The best way is (for each user) to make a copy of either the whole *My Documents* folder or just those folders that you care about (for instance, you may not want to back-up the *My Pictures* folder), on either a floppy disk (one or more) or CD-ROM.

7   You should regularly update this back-up; the safest way is to operate with two sets of back-ups, one that you made (say) a week ago, and one that you made today. You can reuse the oldest set of disks when you make today's back-up. On any day that you make significant or important changes to your documents, make a back-up.

8   Windows® has a back-up utility in *Accessories – System Tools*; this wizard enables you to make back-ups elsewhere on the hard drive, or to a CD-ROM, and also enables you to make a recovery disk that will enable you to recover from a complete crash. You should have a recovery disk. You won't know you need it, until you need it. Then you'll really need it.

9   If your information is particularly critical, you should keep these back-ups offsite – so that, if there is a fire or some other natural disaster, your critical information will survive it.

10 Online, browser-accessible back-up services are now available that should be able to automate and make your back-up easier. This is the route to go, if you have a broadband connection and are working continuously, and therefore need to back-up on a daily (or more frequent) basis.

11 Back-up for notebooks and laptops is also essential. Computers crash. Crashes can be fatal for your device, for the information stored on it and for you. It is true that PDA users suffer from a back-up disaster (i.e. they hadn't got round to it) more often than laptop

users, but that's because PDAs are lost or crashed more often than laptops.

In the mobile computing context, you need to back-up regularly and there is the possible need for recovery while away from the office.

There are basically two approaches to notebook back-up:

i   Provision of a portable (USB or FireWire®) hard drive that has sufficient capacity to handle the *My Documents* folder (with or without *My Pictures* and *My Music*).

- Look for software back-up management options that enable recovery from a hard drive failure or to a replacement laptop – a device such as the Flip2disk from, for example, *www.amacomdirect.co.uk* which provides a full, bootable means of recovery.

- Look for an option that will handle incremental back-ups, which will run on the hard drive, creating and maintaining files of changes which it will upload to remote servers when next the user logs on.

- Look for options that are easy for non-technical people to handle.

- Remember that, whatever product you choose under this option, you could have a lot of valuable, confidential data sitting on an ultra-portable, easy to use device that's designed for fast rendering onto another computer. Data encryption and user authentication are therefore absolutely essential in any portable back-up product that you might choose.

ii The alternative is an online back-up service, of which there are a number. Each has different advantages and there are a variety of pricing plans. Two that work effectively and inexpensively are *www.datadepositbox.com* and *www.pcfort.co.uk*.

- Such services do, however, need to be installed and configured (preferably over a broadband connection with good upload speeds) before you start travelling, as the initial back-up will be time consuming.

- If you use the online back-up service for the *My Documents* folder, you still need to think through how you will restore from a hard drive crash or notebook loss. One approach is to combine an external hard drive (which you could create yourself, remembering to include the all-important boot components and all the latest patches that you've installed to your desktop, or which could be a product such as the Flip2disk), which has a one-time copy of the operating system, applications and the necessary recovery programs but which is not used on a day-to-day basis, with incremental online back-up for daily activity. The right decision on this will be driven by a combination of your budget restrictions, ease of use considerations, and assessment of risks.

CHAPTER 10: RULE 10 – FIX PROBLEMS AS SOON AS THEY ARISE

1   From time to time, something may get past your defences. It might be a virus, worm or Trojan. It might be a hack attack. It might be spyware. Sort the problem out as soon as possible – otherwise it is likely to get worse.

2   Tackle the possible issues step by step:

    i   The first step is to disconnect your computer from your network.

    ii   The next step is to have your anti-virus software run a complete system and disk scan. Close all your programs and run the scan. Wait for, and act on, the results of that scan.

    iii   The scan may identify that you have malware on your system that has bypassed your protective controls. Your anti-virus software might not be able to remove this code, so run the Microsoft® Malicious Software removal tool – available from Microsoft® downloads. It automatically downloads as a monthly security update and runs on your computer, detecting and eliminating any resident (active) malicious software. You might not want to wait for the next monthly update, so download it manually, and let it run and try to detect if you have active malicious code on your computer. Alternatively, if your scan identifies the virus, it might direct you to download a specific removal tool from its own website. Do this. If this doesn't solve your problem, go to the next step.

iv The next step is to carry out a Windows® Defender scan. Have Windows® Defender carry out a full system scan. Wait for, and act on, the results of that scan – which should include removing any adware or spyware on your computer unless you are absolutely certain that you need it. If this doesn't solve your problem, go to the next step.

v The next step is to carry out a broader security audit. The best place to do this is: *www.securityspace.com/sspace/index.html* and run their Free Trial Audit. This will tell you if you have vulnerabilities that a hacker might have exploited and is likely to point to openings in your firewall. This may lead you to increase the security setting of your firewall. Once you have done this, check to see if your computer is behaving properly. If not, there is one final step you can make before you call for outside help.

vi This final step is to restore your system to its configuration prior to the problem. System Restore will reverse ALL changes to Windows® between today and any earlier date you choose, but won't change any data files. It will reverse everything, including updates and patches, so you don't want to have to go too far back – which is why you want to identify and deal with problems as soon as possible.

- *Start – Programs – Accessories – System Tools – System Restore* gets you to the place you want to be. Choose *Restore my computer to an earlier time*, then *Next*, then pick the date immediately before the day on which you think your problem occurred. Click *Next* until you're told to re-start your system, and then re-start it. Hopefully, your problem has now gone.

- You can reverse the system restore process, simply by going through the steps set out above and picking the most current date as the restoration date.

3   If, after doing this, you still have a problem, you should seek professional help.

GLOSSARY

Acceptable Use Policy – an Acceptable Use Policy sets out what your employer considers acceptable behaviour on, and acceptable use of, the company's e-mail and Internet access systems.

Access agreement – this is an agreement, between an organisation and each of its employees, issued prior to release of a specific user name, in which the employee accepts the access rights and privileges attached to that user name and agrees to follow a series of procedures and requirements in respect of the use of that user name.

Administrator – this is the user role that is responsible for installation, configuration, update, amendment or deletion of a system, usually a software system. An administrator can do anything, usually untraceably. It's a powerful computer role.

Adware – advertising that is integrated into software and which is usually provided as a download to a computer in combination with another application provided at no charge on condition that the adware is run. Adware is sometimes malicious.

Anti-malware software – this is software specifically developed to deal with malware: adware, spam, spyware, Trojans, viruses, worms, and most automated exploits, irrespective of their attack vector. This term should not be seen as synonymous with anti-virus software, not all of which adequately copes with the range of ways in which individuals and organisations connect to the Internet. A good anti-virus software package will deal with all malware except for adware and spyware, which may need their own solutions.

Anti-spyware software – is software that will identify spyware packages that are installed on a computer and, if given the instruction by the user, will then remove all instances of them from the computer – wherever they are hiding.

Anti-virus software – Anti-virus software is software that is specifically designed to detect and halt viruses, worms and Trojans in e-mail. It is not necessarily designed to deal with spyware, adware, spam, or anything coming through Instant Messenger.

1   Anti-virus software tackles viruses at three points: it examines incoming e-mail (particularly attachments) at your e-mail gateway for known viruses; it scans the hard disk and all the files for any viruses that may have bypassed the gateway virus checker; and it scans outgoing e-mails to ensure they are not carrying an infection.

2   There are two types of virus detection. The first relies on identifying precise characteristics of viruses (by searching for their 'signatures' and comparing them with its database of known viruses) and the second (heuristic detection) searches for types of misbehaving programs. New worms are more likely to be detected by heuristic checks.

3   Normal viruses are only going to be detected if your anti-virus software has an up-to-date

database of signatures. This means regular updates – daily is better than once per week.

4   Tip: allow the automatic update service to run the moment it alerts you; a large proportion of viruses and other exploits propagate themselves via computers that don't yet have the latest updates installed.

5   Installing more than one anti-virus software package WILL NOT increase your protection – it may even decrease your protection if the packages conflict.

6   Windows® XP Service Pack 2 does not contain anti-virus software. It will alert you if your anti-virus software is not running, or is not up to date, but that is all.

7   Today's blended threats mean that your anti-virus software must integrate with your firewall and other anti-malware software (anti-spam, anti-spyware, Instant Message protection, etc.): unless you are a sophisticated user, you are better off finding and installing a package that covers all the bases rather than attempting to configure a number of different packages from a number of different suppliers to work together; if you current supplier hasn't worked out how to do it, you might just look for one who can.

Applet – is a small Java program that runs in a browser. Applets are designed so that they cannot read or write to the browser's computer file system or open any other network connections.

Application (or application software) – this is the software that users actually use – Microsoft® Office®, or Outlook®, for instance.

Automated hacks – a method of exploiting a vulnerability in software that has been turned into a piece of autonomous code and released onto the Internet.

Automatic updates – a software provider's automated process for issuing updates (patches, fixes and upgrades) to their installed base of users, such that the update is executed with a minimum of user involvement.

Back door – programmers or administrators deliberately leave ways into software systems that can be used later to allow access to the system while bypassing the authorised user file. Sometimes, developers forget to take out something that was put there simply to ease development work or to assist with the debugging routine.

Back-up – a back-up is a copy of information that is made and retained in case of loss or damage to the original – it could be paper copies of paper documents, but we are mostly concerned with digital copies of digital data.

Biometrics – is the identification of a user by means of a physical characteristic, such as a fingerprint, iris, face or voice.

Blacklisting – a list with negative connotations: for instance, it might be a list of those senders that a spam filter will ALWAYS filter out, or a list of those cell phones that will be banned from connecting to the cell phone network.

Blended threat – this might more accurately be described as the threat of a blended attack, an attack which comes from a number of directions, or via a number of vectors. For instance, a spam e-mail message might be carrying a payload, in the form of a Trojan which it installs on your computer to open it up to a botnet. Similarly, an innocent-looking piece of adware might contain some spyware, a Trojan installer and a browser hijacker.

Botnet – this is a network of zombie computers, usually created and controlled by criminals, either for distributing spam or for mounting distributed denial of service attacks.

Browser (Internet Explorer®, Firefox, Opera) – this is the piece of software that enables a user to browse sites on the Web. Microsoft's Internet Explorer® is the most widely used; Firefox and Opera are two open-source competitors.

Cache – this is the section of a computer's memory which retains recently accessed data in order to speed up repeated access to the same data. If the data on the Web has altered since you last visited it, you may need to refresh the page to see the new data; otherwise you will only see what is stored in the cache.

Chat room – a virtual room, on the Web, in which users can chat.

Configuration – how the components of a computer or a network are set up.

Cookie – this is a small data file a website stores on a surfer's computer which contains information about the user (e.g. user preferences) relevant to the user's experience of the website.

CPU – **C**entral **P**rocessor **U**nit – this drives your computer.

Crash – this is what software sometimes does.

Credit cards – pieces of plastic that enable people to get into debt; they are also essential for online shopping.

Credit reports – summary of financial information about consumers assembled on the basis of information filed with credit reporting companies, primarily by lenders.

Cybercrime – any form of illegal activity that takes place in cyberspace. The UK's Computer Misuse Act 1990 made it an offence for anyone to access a computer without authorisation, to modify the contents of a computer without authorisation, or to facilitate (allow) such activity to take place. It identified sanctions for such activity, including fines and imprisonment. Other countries have taken similar action to identify and create offences that should enable law enforcement bodies to deal with computer misuse.

Cyberspace – another term for the digital world, as opposed to the analogue one.

Cyber-terrorism – terrorist activities in cyberspace.

Cyber trust – cyberspace is still an inherently untrustworthy realm, in which it is not possible for buyers and sellers to physically establish one another's bona fides. Methods of establishing cyber trust are therefore essential for effective e-commerce.

Cyber war – this is war in cyberspace, conducted by the military equivalents of hackers, spammers and virus writers.

Dialler – this is software (usually on a website) that will dial out to another website and charge back to you (on a credit card or, more usually, on your existing telephone bill) for the time used while on that site. The charge rate will not necessarily be lower than that of your existing supplier. An auto-dialler will do this without asking your permission – and probably without you knowing about it.

Denial of Service attacks – this sort of attack is designed to put an organisation out of business – or to interrupt the activities of an individual or group of individuals – for a time by freezing its systems. This is usually done by flooding a Web server (or other device) with e-mail messages or other data so that it is unable to provide a normal service to authorised users.

Distributed Denial of Service attack – this uses the computers of other, third party organisations or individuals (which have themselves been commandeered by the hacker) to mount an even larger scale attack on a target.

Encryption – the conversion of plain text into code, using a mathematical algorithm, to prevent it from being read by a third party.

File sharing – the public sharing of files across a network, so that a number of users are able to access and use the same file.

Filter – is a software pattern or mask that is designed so that, some types of items can pass through it while others will be caught and prevented or discarded.

Firewall – is a technology that is designed to create a definite barrier and separation between two parts of a network, or between a network (or individual computer) and the Internet. It filters traffic through its ports in line with its traffic filtering rules, which are set by the computer user (or network administrator).

Flash – an animation technology from Macromedia; it can be watched through a browser.

Flash memory – a non-volatile memory device that retains its data when the power is removed.

Freeware – this is software that is available on the Internet, and can be downloaded for free. This free download may be conditional on you downloading an adware program, which may come bundled with a number of scum ware applications.

Gateway – technically, hardware or software that translates between two dissimilar protocols and, often, any mechanism that provides access from one system to another (e.g. between a network and the Internet).

Hackers – hackers break into computer systems. Unlike crackers, they claim that they get permission first and will publish the results of their 'research'. Hackers have four prime motivations: *challenge*, to solve a security puzzle and outwit an identified security set-up; *mischief*, wanting to inflict stress or damage on an individual or organisation; *working around*, getting around bugs or other blocks in a software system; and *theft*, stealing money or information. Hackers like to talk about 'white hat' and 'black hat' hackers; the argument is that the 'black hat' hackers are malicious and destructive (i.e. 'crackers') while the 'white hat' hackers simply enjoy the challenge and are really on the side of good, offering their skills to help organisations test and defend their networks. This differentiation is convenient for hackers, who seem able to change hats as easily as they evade most network defences. The only sensible approach for any security conscious organisation is to assume that all hackers are potentially in the wrong colour hat, however they might initially present themselves. 'Grey hats' is a term that is evolving to recognise the uncertain danger of so-called 'ethical' hackers. Nowadays, common sense suggests that a hacker of any sort is not to be trusted.

Hard drive – the permanent data storage device built into a workstation that stores the computer's operating system, applications and other software and provides storage for files and folders. Its size is usually expressed in gigabytes.

Hot fixes – are vendor-generated software packages composed of one or more files that address an identified problem or vulnerability.

HTTP – hyper text transfer protocol – a protocol for information transfer across the Web.

https – this is a secure version of **HTTP, using SSL.**

Identity theft – this is when someone gathers enough information about someone else (name, address, data of birth, credit card numbers, social security number, etc.) to successfully impersonate that person online, by mail, over the telephone, or in person.

IP address – a computer address recognisable in IP (Internet Protocol) – the most basic protocol Internet communication.

Java – a programming language from Sun Microsystems that was designed for writing programs (Applets) that include animations, scrolling text, sound effects, games, etc. that can be downloaded from the Web without fear of viruses or other harm to a computer.

JavaScript – a scripting language widely used to create pop-up and pop-under ads, and other functionality, on Web pages.

JPEGs – Joint Photographics Experts Group – a compression technique for colour images and photographs and, therefore, how they are saved. There is a future possibility that JPEG viruses might emerge; these are best resisted by doing the basics consistently.

Keystroke logger – software that records key depressions on a computer keyboard; the software can either be installed on the computer (in which case it can be detected by AntiSpyware software) or it can run inside a secret device attached to the computer, in which case AntiSpyware software will not detect it.

Licence – any software that is being used is potentially subject to copyright restrictions and it is essential that any organisation or user ensures that it has the correct type and number of licences for this software. Microsoft will be restricting upgrade and support services to users of unlicensed (illegal) software.

Malwares any form of 'malicious stuff' that tries to clog up your computer. It includes adware, spam, spim, spyware, viruses, worms, Trojans and automated exploits. Its attack vectors include e-mail attachments, instant messaging, unprotected Internet connections and browsers. You could also call it 'scumware'.

'Man in the middle' – a hacker places himself undetected between two parties to an Internet transaction, whether on a LAN, an unsecured Internet link, a WLAN or on a cellular telephone network. The hacker intercepts and reads messages between the two parties and can alter them without the intended recipient knowing what has happened.

Online payment system – a number of organisations offer third party payment services. The best known are: WorldPay, PayPal, Amazon.com Payments, Yahoo! PayDirect, and VeriSign Inc.

Operating system – this is the software that controls how a computer uses its memory, disk space, folders and files, desktop, etc. Microsoft® Windows® and Apple Macintosh are the two most popular proprietary operating systems. There are also open source operating systems.

Parental control – this is software that is designed to enable parents to scan, filter and control the websites visited by their children, to protect them from objectionable content.

Password cracking – is, on balance, very easy. Most users do not set up passwords or, if they do, they use very simple passwords that they can easily remember, like 'secret' or 'password', or their children's names, or birthdays, sports teams, or particular anniversaries, or family names. While some hackers can quickly identify particular user's passwords, software is now available on the Internet that will apply 'brute force' to automatically, and at high speed, try every theoretically possible alphanumeric combination of user name and password and, usually aided by a dictionary (a 'dictionary attack') of common passwords, this can quickly enable a hacker to gain access to a system. Once a hacker locates the list of encrypted user passwords on the security server or on your hard drive, they can use Internet-available software tools to decrypt it.

Patch – an update to a file that replaces only parts of the file, rather than the whole file.

Payload – the damage or other malicious activity that a virus, worm or spam causes.

Peer- to-peer – a network connecting two or more computers directly to one another, without using a central file server.

Penetration tests – testing whether or not your security defences (firewall, specifically) can be bypassed using any of the known hacking tools and vulnerabilities.

Phishing – sending e-mails that falsely claim to come from a legitimate company in an attempt to scam users into surrendering information that can be used for identity theft.

Pop ups and **pop downs** – small windows that appear when users visit some websites; pop ups are the windows that pop up, pop downs do it in the other direction.

Privacy – the control that individuals (are supposed to) have over the collection, use and distribution of their personal, private information.

Reboot – this is what you have to do after your computer has crashed.

Recycle bin – the Microsoft® desktop folder into which deletions go – and stay, until you remember to go and empty the deleted items folder. Until you empty this folder, any files in it can be dragged back into use.

Retrovirus – a virus that attempts to disable anti-virus software.

Screensaver – a program that displays an image (blank or moving) on a computer screen after the computer has had no input for a period of time – originally designed so that images wouldn't be burned into old CRT screens, they have become entertaining.

Security centre (Windows® XP SP2) – this is the single control point for the Windows® Internet security features, from which the firewall, anti-virus software, automatic update service and Internet options can be controlled. It can be accessed through the Control Panel.

Service packs – are the cumulative product and security software updates (usually including all previous hot fixes, security updates and patches) which need to be downloaded from the supplier's website in order to keep the product up to date.

Shareware – is software that is provided on the basis that, if you like it, you will pay something for it. You can share this software with friends, but they too are expected to make a contribution.

Social engineering attack – this is the easiest and most common method of gaining access to a network, tricking someone into providing confidential information. The hacker, for instance, poses as a network administrator or a fellow employee, with an urgent problem, which can only be resolved by the employee providing confidential information (such as user name or password). Alternatively, the hacker has a false business card, claiming to be a key technical or business support representative, or claims to be a new employee trying to get up to speed in the business. Passwords should NEVER be divulged to anyone, anywhere, for any reason, under any conditions. NOT EVER. This is one of the most important, fundamental and basic security rules.

Spam – this is the unsolicited commercial bulk e-mail, or junk mail. Some of it may be useful, which is why you need to filter it.

Spoofing – IP spoofing gains unauthorised access to a system by masquerading as a valid Internet (IP) address. Web spoofing involves the hacker re-directing traffic from a valid Web address to a fraudulent, look-alike website where customer information (and particularly credit card information) is captured for later illegal reuse – *see also phishing.*

Spyware – is any software that, without your explicit consent, shares information about you with a third party on the Internet.

SSL – is a handshake protocol that provides security and privacy to Internet transactions. SSL was designed to ensure that, even if information is intercepted, it can not be viewed by someone who is not authorised to do so. The default settings in browsers should identify sites that are not secure and should warn that information submitted could be intercepted or observed by a third party. This warning does not appear where there is a valid SSL connection. There are other signs that there is an SSL connection: the URL will change from http to https and a closed padlock will appear in the bar at the bottom of the browser window.

Surf control – this is a software technology that is designed to allow blocking to surfers of particular sites, or groups of sites. Parents can use it to protect their children from offensive or dangerous sites, and organisations can use it to deter their employees from visiting illegal or undesirable sites, or doing other undesirable things.

Trojan – a Trojan is hostile code concealed within and purporting to be bona fide code. It is designed to reach a target stealthily and be executed inadvertently. It may have been installed at the time the software was developed. They can be programs that, while perhaps appearing to be a useful utility, are designed to secretly damage the host system. Some will also try to open up host systems to outside attack.

Uninterruptible Power Source (UPS) – this is a device which is designed to keep other electrically powered devices operating when the normal power supply fails. A UPS should, at the very least, be rated as capable of meeting the power requirements of the device(s) it is supporting for long enough to allow an orderly shutdown of the services. The length of time required for this may need to be ascertained by testing.

URL – **U**niform **R**esource **L**ocator, the address of a website on the World Wide Web.

User name – every user should have a specific and unique name for use on the system or on a computer; in organisations, this name should be created and allocated in line with a standard procedure and should be set up on the system with specific access rights and privileges. The user name has to be created before the user can access the system for the first time.

Virtual Private Networks (VPNs) (SSL, IPSEC) – encrypted and authenticated logical (not physical) links across shared or public networks that provide remote links to an organisational network. A VPN server within the organisational perimeter encrypts data sent to a VPN client outside the perimeter, and vice versa.

Virus – a virus is a piece of computer code that is designed to make your computer sick. Like biological viruses, it indiscriminately selects and infects those whose defences are weak or non-existent. Technically, a virus has at least two properties: it is a program capable of replicating, i.e. producing functional copies of itself, and it depends on a host file (a document or executable file, shared by e-mail or Instant Messenger) to carry each copy. It may or may not have a 'payload', the ability to do something funny or destructive or clever when it arrives.

- There are some 100,000 known viruses in the wild. These range from primitive bits of code written at the dawn of computing time, and from which almost all computers are now completely immune, to more destructive creatures like 2004's MyDoom, Slammer, Sobig (with all its variants) and Bugbear. Up-to-date anti-virus software protects against all of these, without you ever having to know what they do or how they work.

- Viruses exploit software faults (vulnerabilities) to attack computers and their payloads range from silly messages, to individual keys becoming inoperative, to the complete death of your computer.

- The same virus doesn't always have the same name with every anti-virus vendor. This is very irritating and it reflects the fact that the same virus is usually discovered, analysed, reverse engineered and the appropriate anti-virus signature update produced by a number of competitive vendors working in parallel, each of them having allocated the virus their own version of the name.

- Most viruses attack Microsoft products, not just because Microsoft products have flaws (vulnerabilities) but because it is the most widely used computer software in the world, installed on in excess of 90% of desktops. Computer viruses spread by harvesting e-mail address books and forwarding themselves to everyone you know – in an e-mail identified as having come from you – a good way of losing friends and business contacts.

- It's not just Microsoft, though. ALL software has vulnerabilities, even the open source versions.

- And it's not just workstations and computer networks that have virus challenges: increasingly, PDAs and cell phones are coming under attack and, as they too need to carry confidential or valuable data, they also need to be protected.

- Virus writers intend to exploit vulnerabilities in their target software and, as soon as a weakness is identified, the race is on to exploit it – and to see it off. The speed with which new viruses are developed is increasing – it is now only a matter of days between the announcement of a vulnerability and the appearance of the first virus exploiting it.

- A 'zero day' exploit is one in which the exploit is out in the wild on the same day that the vulnerability is announced.

Virus hoax – there are people out there who think it is dead funny to send e-mails to everyone they know, warning of a virus that isn't one. Frankly, if a real or important new virus existed that you had to hear about from some acquaintance rather than from your anti-virus company, you've either chosen a very poor anti-virus supplier (if you have one at all) or you're being hoaxed. If you're reading this book, chances are it'll be the latter. *http://vmyths.com/index.cfm* is a good place to go if you really want to be sure that a message you've received is a hoax.

Virus writers – 'people' who write viruses; they should be taken outside and have unspeakable things done to them. Mostly, they are sad people who do it for fun and because they enjoy the challenge of writing clever code. Sometimes they do it out of loneliness, or because they want to have some impact on the world. They often work together and have online groups, websites and communities through which they share work and ideas. They also compete with one another and certainly their relationship with anti-virus companies is often extremely hostile. Virus toolkits are available online, so that anyone with limited code writing skills can also create a virus.

Vulnerability – this is a weakness of an asset or group of assets that can be exploited by a threat. There are regularly updated central stores of known vulnerabilities at Bugtraq and CVE and in the SANS top 20.

War dialling – a computer program (usually freeware or shareware) used by hackers to identify phone numbers that can connect to a computer modem. The program automatically dials a defined range of phone numbers and records in a database those numbers that connect successfully. Some programs can also identify the computer's operating system and may also conduct automated penetration testing by running through a predetermined list of common user names and passwords in an attempt to gain access to the system.

Whitelist – is the list of people that you positively want to receive e-mails from.

WiFi – Wireless Fidelity – is the name given to wireless networking that meets a number of standards promulgated by the IEEE. Those most commonly encountered are 802.11a, 802.11b (the original WiFi), 802.11g and 802.11i.

Worm – unlike a virus, a worm is autonomous. It does not rely upon a host file to carry it. It can replicate itself (i.e. is self-propagating), which it does by means of a transmission medium such as e-mail, Instant Messaging, Internet Relay Chat, network connections, etc. Polymorphic worms are capable of evolving in the wild, so that they can more effectively overcome evolving virus defences.

Zombie – this, as you might expect, is a once independent computer that is now under the discretionary, malign control of another computer somewhere else in the world. A remote user can take advantage of inadequate anti-virus and firewall defences to install remote control software on other computers. This remote control software enables the remote user to use your computer – without you even being aware of it – for the mass forwarding of spam or as part of a massive, coordinated attack on another website – a Distributed Denial of Service attack.

FURTHER READING

Blocking Spam and Spyware for Dummies, Peter Gregory, Mike Simon, Wiley Publishing Inc. (2005).

Caution! Music and Video Downloading: Your Guide to Legal, Safe and Trouble-Free Downloads, Russell Shaw, J Wiley Inc. (2004).

Computer Viruses for Dummies, Peter Gregory, Wiley Publishing Inc. (2004).

The Everyday Internet All-in-one Desk Reference for Dummies, Peter Weverka, Wiley Publishing Inc. (2005).

Firewalls For Dummies, 2nd Edition, Brian Komar, Ronald Beekelarr & Joern Wettern, Wiley Publishing Inc. (2003).

Home Networking for Dummies, 3rd Edition, Kathy Ivens, Wiley Publishing Inc. (2005).

Internet Privacy for Dummies, John R Levine, Ray Everett-Church, Greg Stebben, David Lawrence, Wiley Publishing Inc. (2002).

Preventing Identity Theft for Dummies, Michael Arata, Wiley Publishing Inc. (2004).

Secrets & Lies: Digital Security in a Networked World, Bruce Schneier, Wiley Computer Publishing (2004).

Troubleshooting your PC for Dummies, Dan Gookin, Wiley Publishing Inc. (2005).

Further Reading

Wireless Home Networking for Dummies, Danny Briere, Walter Bruce III, Pat Hurley, Wiley Publishing Inc. (2003).

Wireless Networks for Dummies, Barry D. Lewis & Peter T. Davis, Wiley Publishing Inc (2004).

USEFUL WEBSITES

IT Governance Ltd (the company)

www.itgovernance .co.uk

Blogspot

http://alancalder.blogspot.com

Microsoft

www.microsoft.com

www.microsoft.com/technet/default.asp

www.microsoft.com/downloads

Microsoft Security Centre

www.microsoft.com/technet/security/default.mspx

Others

Anti-phishing Working Group

www.antiphishing.org

Information Commissioner

www.informationcommissioner.gov.uk

UK NISCC Advice Centre for Internet Users

www.itsafe.gov.uk

Virus Myths

http://vmyths.com/index.cfm

WiFi Alliance

www.wi-fi.org

ITG RESOURCES

IT Governance Ltd source, create and deliver products and services to meet the real-world, evolving IT governance needs of today's organisations, directors, managers and practitioners. The ITG website (_www.itgovernance.co.uk_) is the international one-stop-shop for corporate and IT governance information, advice, guidance, books, tools, training and consultancy.

_www.itgovernance.co.uk/bc_dr.aspx_ is the ITG website that includes a comprehensive range of books, tools and document templates for business continuity, disaster recovery and BS25999.

www.27001.com is the IT Governance Ltd website that deals specifically with information security issues in a North American context.

Pocket Guides

For full details of the entire range of Pocket Guides listed below, simply follow the links at _www.itgovernance.co.uk/publishing.aspx_.

Toolkits

ITG's unique range of toolkits includes the IT Governance Framework Toolkit, which contains all the tools and guidance that you will need in order to develop and implement an appropriate IT governance framework for your organisation. Full details can be found at _www.itgovernance.co.uk/products/519_.

For a free paper on how to use the proprietary CALDER-MOIR IT Governance Framework, and for a free trial version of the toolkit, see _www.itgovernance.co.uk/calder_moir.aspx_.

Best Practice Reports

ITG's new range of Best Practice Reports is now at: _www.itgovernance.co.uk/best-practice-reports.aspx_.
These offer you essential, pertinent, expertly researched information on an increasing number of key issues.

Training and Consultancy

IT Governance also offer training and consultancy services across the entire spectrum of disciplines in the information governance arena. Details of training courses can be accessed at _www.itgovernance.co.uk/training.aspx_ and descriptions of our consultancy services can be found at _www.itgovernance.co.uk/consulting.aspx_.

Why not contact us to see how we could help you and your organisation?

Newsletter

IT governance is one of the hottest topics in business today, not least because it is also the fastest moving, so what better way to keep up than by subscribing to ITG's free monthly newsletter _Sentinel_? It provides monthly updates and resources across the whole spectrum of IT governance subject matter, including risk management, information security, ITIL and IT service management, project governance, compliance and so much more. Subscribe for your free copy at: _www.itgovernance.co.uk/newsletter.aspx_.